Cheetahs

By Ethan Grucella

Gareth Stevens
Publishing

Please visit our Web site, www.garethstevens.com. For a free color catalog of all our high-quality books, call toll free 1-800-542-2595 or fax 1-877-542-2596.

Library of Congress Cataloging-in-Publication Data

Grucella, Ethan.
Cheetahs / Ethan Grucella.
     p. cm. – (Animals that live in the grasslands)
Includes index.
ISBN 978-1-4339-3864-1 (pbk.)
ISBN 978-1-4339-3865-8 (6-pack)
ISBN 978-1-4339-3863-4 (library binding)
1. Cheetah–Juvenile literature. I. Title.
QL737.C23G79 2011
599.75'9–dc22

                                        2010004566

First Edition

Published in 2011 by
Gareth Stevens Publishing
111 East 14th Street, Suite 349
New York, NY 10003

Designer: Michael J. Flynn
Editor: Therese Shea

Photo credits: Cover, pp. 1, 5, 7, 13, 15, 17, 19, 21, back cover Shutterstock.com; p. 9 Heinrich van den Berg/Gallo Images/Getty Images; p. 11 David Higgs/Taxi/ Getty Images.

Printed in the United States of America

CPSIA compliance information: Batch #CS10GS: For further information contact Gareth Stevens, New York, New York at 1-800-542-2595.

Table of Contents

Boldface words appear in the glossary.

The Winner!

Which animal could win any race on land? A cheetah! Cheetahs are the fastest land animals. They can be found in the **grasslands** of Africa.

5

Built for the Hunt

A cheetah has a yellow body, black spots, and a white stomach. It also has black lines on its face. It looks like it is crying!

black line

black spots

Cheetahs are built to run. They are thin with long legs. They have claws and pads on their feet. These help them dig into the ground as they run.

claw

pad

A cheetah's **lungs** and heart keep it running fast. A cheetah may take 150 breaths a minute when it is running!

Looking for a Meal

Cheetahs are meat eaters. They hunt animals such as birds, rabbits, and **antelope**. A cheetah can see far. It may wait in high places for **prey**.

First, a cheetah creeps close to its prey. Then, it runs as fast as 70 miles (113 km) an hour. The cheetah knocks down the animal and bites it.

Cheetahs are tired after running so fast. They may rest before they eat. During this time, other animals may try to take their food.

Cheetah Cubs

A mother cheetah may have two to eight cubs at one time. The cubs hide in the tall grass until they can run and hunt.

cub

When the cubs are around 2 years old, their mother leaves them. **Male** cheetahs join a group with other males. **Females** may stay near their mother.

Fast Facts

Height	about 30 inches (76 centimeters) at the shoulder
Length	about 80 inches (203 centimeters) from head to tail
Weight	between 85 and 140 pounds (40 to 65 kilograms)
Diet	small and medium-sized animals, such as birds, rabbits, and antelope
Average life span	about 7 years in the wild

Glossary

antelope: a four-legged animal with hoofs and horns that lives in Africa and Asia

female: a girl

grasslands: land on which grass is the main kind of plant life

lung: a body part that helps animals breathe

male: a boy

prey: an animal hunted as food by another animal

For More Information

Books

Clarke, Ginjer L. *Cheetah Cubs.* New York, NY: Grosset & Dunlap, 2007.

Eckart, Edana. *Cheetah.* New York, NY: Children's Press, 2005.

Web Sites

Cheetah

www.awf.org/content/wildlife/detail/cheetah
See many photos and read interesting facts about cheetahs and other African animals.

Cheetahs

kids.nationalgeographic.com/Animals/CreatureFeature/Cheetah
A map, printouts, and video tell you more about a cheetah's life.

Index

About the Author

Though a practicing physician like his parents, Ethan Grucella is an amateur zoologist with an enthusiasm for African animals. He lives in Cleveland, Ohio, where he writes wildlife books in his spare time.